The Special Stories Series

First Place

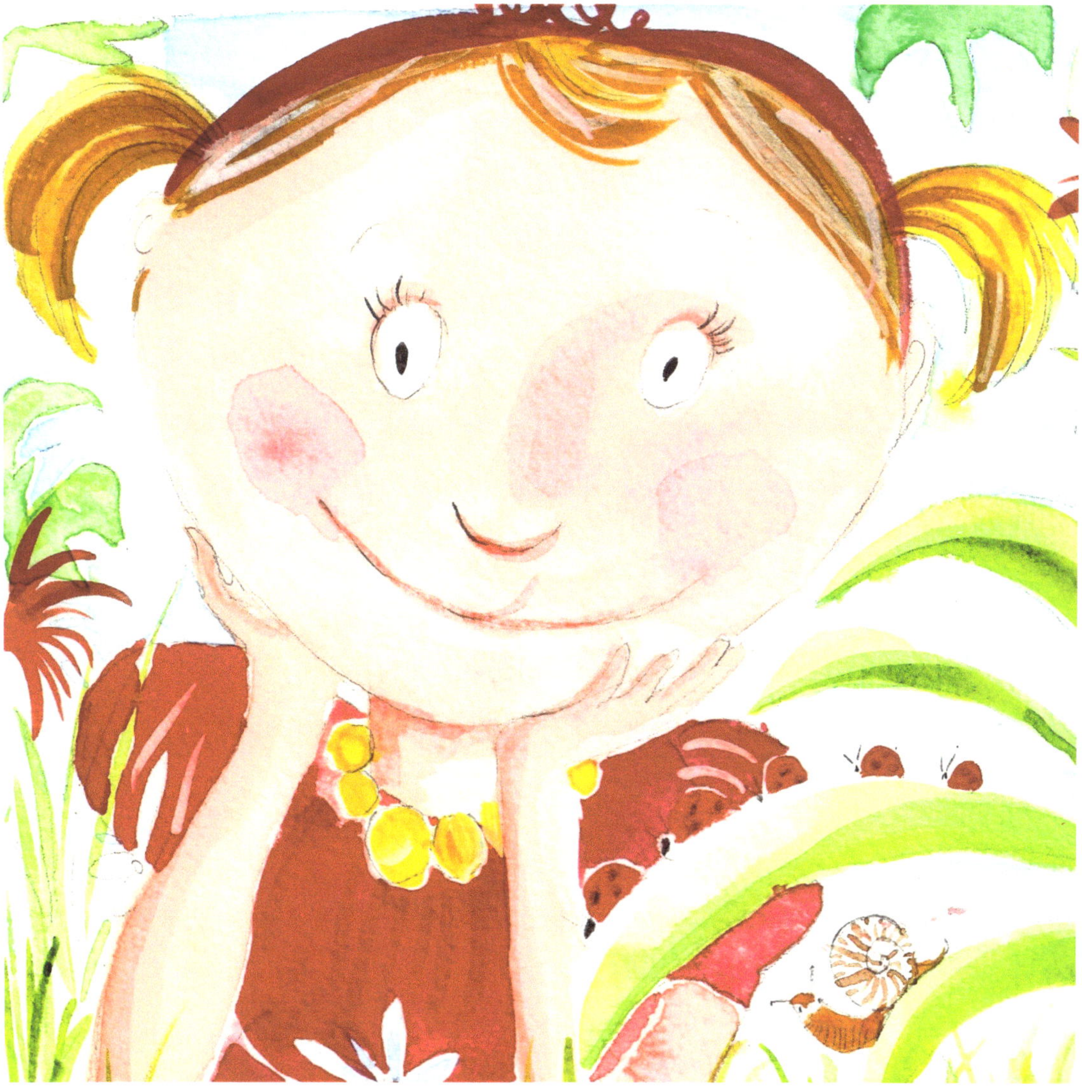

by KATE GAYNOR

illustrated by EVA BYRNE

Published in 2008 by

SPECIAL STORIES PUBLISHING

ISBN 978-0-9555787-6-2

A catalogue record for this book is available from the British Library

Special Stories Publishing

www.specialstories.net

Acknowledgements

Many thanks to Kieran, my father Michael, my brother George and my extended family and friends. Special thanks too to my uncle Liam Gaynor, Liz O'Donoghue, Eva Byrne and the Louth County Enterprise Board for their endless encouragement, support and invaluable advice.

A very special thanks to Tara Cunningham M.D., Jennifer Wetter MS, CCC-SLP, Director of Speech and Language Therapy and Debbie Brassell, Director of Research all at Release Communication Intervention, Dollymount, Dublin 3. www.release.ie

Special thanks also to Dr. Gerard Molloy Ph.D C.Psychol. whose time and effort with this project was so greatly appreciated.

About the Illustrator

Eva Byrne is a well-known illustrator of books such as "Food to Match Your Mood" "Being You" and "So New York". As well as illustrating book covers, newspaper and magazine articles, she has worked on numerous advertising campaigns both in Europe and the United States. She was delighted to be asked to participate in this very special project with Kate Gaynor.

To read more about the special stories collection, visit the Special Stories website at:
www.specialstories.net

for my uncle Liam

Hi! my name is **Lizzy**. I am five years old.

I have three orange goldfish called Dory, Donnie and Dora who live in a big bowl in my bedroom. They don't have much to say, but I think they're just great!

Some boys and girls I know are a little bit like my three goldfish.
We can find talking or speaking pretty hard to do.

Some of us find our letters hard to say and some find it hard to say any words at all. Then there are others, like me, who have something called a cleft palate.

For boys and girls like my friends and I there are some special things we do that other boys and girls don't.

One of these things is going to visit a very special type of teacher who helps us learn how we can be better at talking and speaking.

My special teacher is called Susan. She sometimes wears glasses on her happy smiley face. Even though I have to visit her a lot, I don't mind at all!

Susan says that there are lots of children, even older ones, who have problems trying to talk to others. She also says when children work especially hard at their exercises that it really makes a difference to the way that they speak.

One day at my school, my teacher, Miss White, announced that something very exciting called a talent competition was going to happen at the end of the year.

This is when all the children in the whole school, can stand on stage in the school hall and say a poem or sing a song. Whoever says the best poem or sings the best song could win a prize.

10

Miss White said that children would have to practise very hard if they wanted to be in the talent competition. And that only the very best poems or songs could enter.

That day after school, my mum and I went to visit my special teacher Susan. I told her all about the school talent competition and how I would really like to be on stage with the other boys and girls.

12

Susan told me that if I wanted to say a poem I would have to
work very hard and practise my exercises every day.

I promised Susan that I would. And over the next few months I worked my hardest to practise my words the way Susan had taught me to.

When the day of the school talent competition arrived, I was the very last girl on to the stage to say my poem. But just before I began to speak, I suddenly felt afraid that the other children might not like how I would say my poem…

But instead of running away, I marched out onto the stage and said my poem the very best that I could, even though some of the words were hard to say.

When it was over I couldn't believe my eyes. Everyone stood up
and started clapping and cheering and saying that of all the boys
and girls in the talent competition I was the very best!

My teacher came out on to the stage with a big golden trophy just for me. I had won first place in the talent competition! It was a happy, happy day!

18

Since that day, I have always practised my words and my exercises for Susan and my mum and dad and have never been afraid just to try my very best.

If some days my exercises feel like hard work, I just look at my big golden trophy and remember the day when I won first place! So what about you? Do you have a special story like mine? Why don't you tell me all about it on your Special Story Page?

Your Special Story Page

SPECIAL STORIES PUBLISHING
Kate Gaynor

Notes for Grown Ups on Speech and Language Therapy

Some of the most common reasons for communication difficulties in young children:

Cleft lip and cleft palate: A cleft lip or cleft palate results from the incomplete development of the structure of the mouth in the early stages of pregnancy. A cleft lip is a separation of the upper lip and a cleft palate is an opening in the roof of the mouth.

Stammering: Primarily characterised by repetitions, pauses, and prolongations in speech.

Dyspraxia: A disorder that affects the child's ability to easily learn the muscle movements required for speech.

Autism: A condition that affects the normal development of the brain in areas of social interaction and communication.

Down's Syndrome: Caused by a chromosomal arrangement that often results in degrees of developmental delay and certain recognisable characteristics.

Articulation Delays/Disorder: A speech impairment characterized by a person's inability to produce speech sounds correctly, such as lisping or rhotacism (the inability to pronounce the letter 'r').

The assessment, diagnosis and treatment of speech and language disorders require a high level of scientific knowledge and clinical skill. A speech and language therapist is a professionally qualified person who works with children and adults of all ages who have difficulty communicating. Most children who work closely with their therapist will find a significant improvement in communication ability through time.

How to use this book:

Children with cleft palate or any child with speech or language difficulties can feel very isolated and confused as to why they cannot communicate as their peers do. This book helps children realize that many other children just like them have to contend with similar speech difficulties. Through the main character, children learn that they can overcome their speech problems by working closely with their speech therapist and not being afraid to try. The book also gives parents an opportunity to discuss any feelings or anxieties that the child may have as regards their speech difficulty.

For further information about speech and language therapy contact your local association.

Other books from Special Stories Publishing

A FAMILY FOR SAMMY: The purpose of this book is to help explain the foster care process to young children.

JOE'S SPECIAL STORY: This story was written to help explain inter-country adoption to young children.

THE BRAVEST GIRL IN SCHOOL: The objective of this story is to help children with diabetes to appreciate the importance of taking their insulin injections and being aware of what they eat.

THE WINNER: The intention of this book is to help explain Asthma and its effects to young children.

THE FAMOUS HAT: The goal of this book is to help children with leukaemia (or other forms of cancer) to prepare for treatment, namely chemotherapy, and a stay in hospital.

THE LOST PUPPY: This book has been designed to help children with limited mobility to see the positive aspects that using a wheelchair can bring to their lives.

To read more about the special stories collection, visit the Special Stories website at:
www.specialstories.net